WHAT OTHER SCRIPTURE JOURNEY PARTICIPANTS HAVE TO SAY...

"Just as soaking up the sun can give you a healthy tan (and much needed Vitamin D!), soaking up God's truth gives us healthy minds and hearts. It's a spiritual bath to understand the arc of each book of the Bible, but then dive deep to revel in the particulars. I love the way Keith guides us into the light and warmth of God's truth." Gary Thomas (Speaker and Best-Selling Author of *Sacred Marriage* and *Authentic Faith*)

"Has your Bible reading time become stale, aimless, and scattered? God can use the Scripture Journey series to not only to transform your understanding of the Bible, but far more importantly, to draw you into a more personal relationship with God. Now is the perfect time to discover a fresh, consistent, and deeper approach to spending time with God through His Word! Take this journey. You won't regret it." Dr. Rob Rienow (Co-Founder, Visionary Family Ministries)

"Approaching eight decades, I have used many Bible study plans. But Keith Ferrin's approach to saturate your mind and spirit with Scripture is simplicity at its best!" Judith Maxwell

"I highly recommend Keith's Bible studies for both group and personal study. Looking at the whole book to get the big picture before focusing on the individual parts and details gives a completely different perspective. Not to mention looking at verses in context helps give a more accurate understanding." Serene Mendicino

"I loved the Scripture Journey. Opened my eyes to truths I have not seen before." Jim Jacobs

"I really enjoy studying the Bible this way! We read, re-read, and really absorbed the whole book before digging into the details. It helped me get a glimpse of God's bigger picture. Plus, when we shifted to looking at the details, what I learned stuck with me so much more, since I had laid such a good foundation. Thank you, Keith!" Tanya Quakenbush

"Reading the Bible was something I felt I 'had' to do as a Christian, but it did not come alive as God's Word to me until I started reading it with a relational mindset. Now, every day, I am excited to see what God is going to say to me, even if I have read the same words 100 times. This approach changed my life!" Vicki Berg

"I am loving the studies in the Scripture Journey Series. Each one allows me to go back in time with the Holy Spirit-inspired writers of the Scriptures. Paul's life in particular, and his personal walk with the Lord has helped me develop a more intimate relationship with Jesus, my Savior and with God the Father and with the Holy Spirit. I now enjoy my own personal journey into the pages of the Bible more than ever." Sheri Green

PHILIPPIANS SCRIPTURE JOURNEY

A 40-DAY BIBLE STUDY THROUGH THE BOOK OF PHILIPPIANS

KEITH FERRIN

keithferrin.com

KEITH FERRIN PRODUCTIONS

Copyright © 2024 by Keith Ferrin

Published by Keith Ferrin Productions

Unless otherwise noted, The Holy Bible, Berean Standard Bible, BSB is produced in cooperation with Bible Hub, Discovery Bible, OpenBible.com, and the Berean Bible Translation Committee. This text of God's Word has been dedicated to the public domain.

Scripture quotations marked CSB have been taken from the Christian Standard Bible®, Copyright © 2017 by Holman Bible Publishers. Used by permission. Christian Standard Bible® and CSB® are federally registered trademarks of Holman Bible Publishers.

Scripture quotations marked NLT are taken from the Holy Bible, New Living Translation, copyright © 1996, 2004, 2015 by Tyndale House Foundation. Used by permission of Tyndale House Publishers, Inc., Carol Stream, Illinois 60188. All rights reserved.

Scripture quotations marked NIV are taken from The Holy Bible, New International Version® NIV®. Copyright © 1973, 1978, 1984, 2011 by Biblica, Inc. Used with permission. All rights reserved worldwide.

Back cover photo: Scott Yamamura, Created to Create, Seattle, WA

Cover Design: Robert Calvin Williams III, www.ilovemycover.com

ISBN: 9798335480291

All rights reserved. Written permission must be secured from the publisher to use or reproduce any part of this book, except for brief quotations in critical reviews or articles.

For information or to schedule author appearances:

Keith Ferrin

www.keithferrin.com/speaking

keith@keithferrin.com

Dedication

To the members of the *BibleLife Community*.

Back in 2020, the world shut down, 95% of my live events were cancelled and I invited you to join me to study the Bible online. Our very first study was *Philippians*. Here we are, more than four years later, studying this book together.

Philippians is all about the joy of partnership in ministry. Thank you for partnering with me.

Alongside,
Keith

Contents

Introduction	X
How to Use This Book	XII
1. Day 1	1
2. Day 2	4
3. Day 3	7
4. Day 4	10
5. Day 5	13
6. Day 6	16
7. Day 7	19
8. Day 8	21
9. Day 9	23
10. Day 10	26
11. Day 11	29
12. Day 12	32
13. Day 13	35
14. Day 14	38

15. Day 15   40
16. Day 16   43
17. Day 17   46
18. Day 18   49
19. Day 19   52
20. Day 20   55
21. Day 21   58
22. Day 22   60
23. Day 23   63
24. Day 24   66
25. Day 25   69
26. Day 26   72
27. Day 27   75
28. Day 28   78
29. Day 29   81
30. Day 30   84
31. Day 31   87
32. Day 32   90
33. Day 33   93
34. Day 34   96
35. Day 35   99
36. Day 36   102
37. Day 37   105
38. Day 38   108
39. Day 39   111
40. Day 40   114

About the Author	117
A Few of My Other Books	118
Bible Toolbox	122
Let's Connect!	124
Fullpage image	126
Fullpage image	127

Introduction

Back in 1993, when I was a youth and worship pastor at a small, new church in Tacoma, Washington, I saw Bruce Kuhn "perform" the *Gospel of Luke*. It was more powerful than I could put into words.

He agreed to have lunch with me the next day. During that lunch (which turned into an entire afternoon and evening) he challenged me to pick a book and soak in it until I knew it. I took him up on his challenge. That summer, I read *Philippians* every day.

Those two months changed my life. I made connections I had never made. I enjoyed it more than any Bible study I had done in the previous 20 years. I understood what I was reading. I enjoyed what I was reading. I remembered what I was reading. In fact, I got to the end of the summer and realized that I pretty much knew the entire book.

I hadn't just "memorized" it. I had "internalized" it! Philippians was now a part of me.

Just as those two months changed me, I pray that the next several weeks change you!

Paul writes this short letter from prison. He also uses the word "joy" or "rejoice" more times per chapter than any book in the Bible. From prison! Knowing Christ, and the partnership he had with the Christians in Philippi made Paul's joy overflow. As you read and study *Philippians,* may your joy overflow!

Grab your Bible and join me for the *Philippians Scripture Journey.*

Alongside,

How to Use This Book

As I wrote the *Philippians Scripture Journey* (and each of the Bible studies in the *Scripture Journey Series*), my goal was always to make this both helpful and easy-to-use for individuals, families, small groups or Sunday School classes, or any group gathering to read and discuss God's Word.

For Individuals

Each day you will find guidance on what to read in your Bible. I don't print the actual passages in this book because part of going on a *Scripture Journey* is being in your Bible!

After the daily Bible reading, you will find a section called *For Reflection & Discussion*. In this section you will find questions, thoughts to ponder, or ideas for digging deeper.

Finally, at the end of each day I have a page for *Notes & Prayers*. Some Scripture journey-goers find this page helpful for jotting down ideas, thoughts, prayers, or even words or themes you want to explore more deeply after completing the *Philippians Scripture Journey*. Others choose to use a separate journal or digital notebook (especially if you're reading a digital version rather than the physical book) for more thorough reflection, note-taking, or journaling.

One Recommendation: While using the *Philippians Scripture Journey* as an individual is certainly beneficial, to get the most out of the journey – and have more fun doing it! – I highly recommend finding at least one friend to discuss what you are discovering.

For Families

I love doing *Scripture Journeys* with my wife and kids! Depending on the ages of your children, you might need to adjust the *For Reflection & Discussion* section. Add some extra questions, leave some questions out, or put them in your own words. After all, you know your kids way better than I do!

You might also want to decide ahead of time what a realistic timeframe is for your family to go on the *Philippians Scripture Journey*. You will notice that I laid it out for 40 days. I have intentionally left out any spaces for dates, weeks, or months.

If your family reads the Bible together every day...terrific! Make it 40 days. If five days each week is more realistic with your current schedule, tell your kids you're going on an 8-Week Scripture Journey. Three or four days each week can be a 10-Week or 12-Week Scripture Journey. These last few options leave the weekends for "catching up" if you need to!

Remember...This is *relational* time. It is not just about learning something or "getting through" the daily reading. God's desire – and design – is for us to be in relationship. Relationship with Him. Relationship with each other.

For Small Groups and Sunday School Classes

While some small group studies (or classes) are designed in a way that participants don't need to do much during the week, that is not the case for the *Philippians Scripture Journey*. The discussion is only going to flow if participants are spending time during the week "traveling alone" on the journey, with the small group or class time as a place for discussing what each person noticed on their journey.

That said, I encourage you to talk through this at the beginning and agree on how long the journey will be. As with families, this can be 40 days or 8, 10, or 12 weeks. From past *Scripture Journeys* I have done with groups, I have found the best experiences are either an 8-Week or 10-Week journey. (Four or five days of reading each week.)

Since the *For Reflection & Discussion* section is printed right in the book, there is no need for a "leader's guide" or "participant's guide." Each person has the same book. (I like simple!)

DAY 1

Welcome to Day 1 of the *Philippians Scripture Journey*! I am so excited for the journey you are about to go on. *Philippians* is one of the "Prison Epistles." As Paul sits in prison, chained to a wall, he uses the words *"joy"* and *"rejoice"* more times per chapter than in any other book in the entire Bible!

Why? Because of the God who was ever-present with him. And because of the *people* he's writing to. When he thinks of the partnership, friendship, and generosity, he can't help but smile. I pray that you sense Paul's joy as you read his words.

Before diving in, I want to give you a bit of a "roadmap" for the journey ahead. You can think of these 40 days like a Broadway play. You can watch the whole play. You can see how it is broken down into "acts." And each act is broken down even further into "scenes."

- The first 15 days we will read the whole letter. (Watch the "play.")

- Days 16-19 we will focus on a chapter each day. (Explore each of the four "acts.")

- Days 20-35 we will explore a selection of verses. (Dive into each "scene" of *Philippians*.)

- Days 36-39 we will expand to a chapter each day.

- Day 40 we will revisit *Philippians* in its entirety.

Ok. Enough setup. Are you ready to begin the *Philippians Scripture Journey*? For today...it is really complicated. (wink)

Today's Passage: Read *Philippians*

Yup...that's it. Pray before you start, asking – and expecting – God to meet you as you read His Word. Read *Philippians*...out loud...in a *physical Bible*. Why a physical Bible? It's all about distractions vs. focus. I am not against digital Bibles. Having a Bible app on your phone or tablet can be a wonderful resource. But not as your *main* Bible. Here is my reasoning in a nutshell.

> *"Few things are more distracting than holding something in your hand that can do 1,000 things. Few things will help you focus more than holding something that can only do one."*

Ready? Set? Read!

For Reflection & Discussion

- What are your first impressions?
- What hopes do you have for this journey?
- Spend some time asking God to guide you on the journey, as well as bring His Word to your mind throughout each day (not only when you are reading).

Notes & Prayers

Day 2

Today's Passage: Read *Philippians*...out loud.

This first week or two, each day is going to be somewhat similar. **Remember: We're watching the play.** Grasping the storyline. Building a foundation. Laying the groundwork. This is the time for you to leave the notes, study Bibles, and commentaries aside. (We'll get to that soon enough.)

Simply read.

You and your Heavenly Father.

Let Him remind you of His truths, His presence, and His hope for you today.

For Reflection & Discussion

- Write down one verse that stood out to you today. Read that verse five times right now. Set an alarm on your phone for three different times throughout the day. (I call this the *3 Reminders Habit*.)

- When the alarm goes off, read that verse again. See if – and how – it applies to that particular moment.

- If you are meeting with others to discuss the *Philippians Scripture Journey*, part of your discussion can be to share with each other the experience you had with the *3 Reminders Habit*.

Notes & Prayers

Day 3

Read *Philippians*...as if you were Paul, sitting in prison, writing to fellow Christians.

Imagine it. Prison walls. No timeline. He believes he will get out. He hopes and prays he will get out. But for now, it's about waiting. Only waiting.

Waiting is hard. Trusting God's timing is hard. It was hard for Paul. It's hard for us. And yet, God frequently uses our waiting to shape our character. And always remember this...

> *"God cares significantly more about your character than your comfort."*

As you read, do your best to put yourself in Paul's place. Waiting. Hoping. Praying.

For Reflection & Discussion

- How are the words of *Philippians* different as you read through Paul's lens?

- Think of a time when you suffered unjustly? How did you handle it? What was the outcome?

- Have you ever experienced a season of "waiting?" What did God teach you through that season?

- What challenges or encourages you as you read today?

Notes & Prayers

Day 4

Today's Passage: Read *Philippians* (out loud) in a different translation.

If you own a physical Bible in a different translation than your primary one...grab it. If not, open up the YouVersion Bible app or and you'll find plenty of translations to choose from.

Here are the ones I personally like to read throughout the first few weeks: (Choose a few.)

- Berean Standard Bible
- Christian Standard Bible
- New Living Translation
- English Standard Version
- New International Version
- King James Version (or the New King James Version)
- The Message (This is a paraphrase, rather than a translation)

You might be wondering why I am encouraging you to read out loud. It's quite simple actually. When we read out loud, we naturally read with more emotion, which makes it easier to focus. Not only that, but we also remember what we both see *and* hear significantly more than what we *only* see or *only* hear.

Many people feel strange reading the Bible out loud to themselves. However, most people who stick with it for a week or two find it so beneficial for focus and retention, they end up reading the Bible out loud the rest of their lives!

For Reflection & Discussion

- What stood out to you as you read *Philippians* in a different translation?

- Did you notice anything you hadn't noticed before as you read *Philippians* out loud?

- What phrases or words did you notice?

- Are you seeing any themes woven throughout *Philippians*?

Notes & Prayers

DAY 5

Today's Passage: Read *Philippians* and do an *Author* background study.

Almost any Bible teacher will tell you, "*Context is key.*" Throughout these first 15 days, I would encourage you to do three different Background Studies

- The Author – Who wrote the book?
- The Audience – To whom was the book written?
- The Atmosphere – What was happening at that time (in the culture, for the author, and for the audience)?

For some people, Background Studies will become a bit of a hobby. I know people who spend hours reading, researching, and discovering all kinds of interesting background information. If that's you...wonderful! If not...even 10-15 minutes spent discovering a bit more about the context will make your reading richer and more fruitful.

I often think of it like going to a live concert where the musician tells you "The story behind the song." Knowing where the song came from changes the way you listen to it for years to come. The same is true with the Bible.

If you own a study Bible, there is probably some background info in there about Paul. If you don't, you can go to a free Bible study site – like *BibleHub* or *BlueLetterBible* – and find out more about him. You can also ask a friend or pastor what resources they recommend. [1]

For Reflection & Discussion

- How do Paul's situation and background encourage you?

- How does it comfort you?

- How does it challenge you?

- What is one thing you learned about Paul from your research you didn't already know?

Notes & Prayers

Day 6

Today's Passage: Read *Philippians*...as if you were Paul, writing to friends or family members who are far away.

This is similar to the exercise from Day 3. As you think of friends in different areas, you will notice different verses, paragraphs, or themes that you hadn't noticed before. Putting yourself in someone else's shoes will get you out of an entirely me-centered practice of Bible reading.

If you are having a difficult time thinking of someone specific, feel free to come back to this exercise another day. You might find it helpful to simply think about the different "scenes" of your own life. Pick one part of your life – a specific relationship, your work situation, your school situation, or a challenge you're facing – and read *Philippians* while you have that scene in your mind's eye.

For Reflection & Discussion

- What did you notice that you hadn't before?

- Who is another friend (or "scene") you want to jot down so you can do this exercise again?

- Is there something specific you can pray for or share with your friend?

Notes & Prayers

Day 7

Today's Passage: Read *Philippians*.

During these first several days, the priority is reading and "soaking" in *Philippians*. It is not about deep study. It is not about taking a bunch of notes.

It is about reading. Noticing. Enjoying. Sitting with God and letting Him speak to you through His Word.

As you read *Philippians* today, notice one word, phrase, or concept that is new or fresh for you today.

For Reflection & Discussion

- Spend some time meditating on the word, phrase or concept that was new or fresh to you today.

- How might you turn it into a prayer? What else are you noticing as you read and pray?

- Ask God to bring His Word to your mind throughout your day.

Notes & Prayers

Day 8

Today's Passage: Read *Philippians* and write a one-paragraph summary.

This is *not* meant to be overwhelming. You have now read *Philippians* at least eight times. If a friend asked you, *"What's Philippians about?"* how would you answer? How would you put this letter in your own words?

Taking the time to write a few sentences giving an overview of *Philippians* will help solidify the message in your mind. As you go through other *Scripture Journeys,* these one-paragraph summaries will also be a quick way to remind yourself of what is contained in each book you have studied.

For Reflection & Discussion

You might need more than the space provided. Feel free to write in a journal, or take some extra sheets of paper, write your paragraph, and keep your notes tucked in this book to visit at another time. (Looking back even a few years from now at what God was telling you today could be quite eye-opening!)

Notes & Prayers

Day 9

Today's Passage: Read *Philippians* in another translation (different from the one you read on Day 4).

As you begin, pray that God would be present with you as you read. Let Him know you are thankful for the words you are about to read. Ask Him to show you what is true about who He is, what He has done, and who you are because of these truths.

Ask Him to help you focus. When you finish, ask Him to bring His Word to your mind throughout your day.

Then *expect* that He will...and listen! You can even use the *3 Reminders Habit* from Day 2 to start the process of training your mind to return to God's Word throughout the day.

For Reflection & Discussion

- What stood out to you as you read *Philippians* in a third translation?

- Are there any phrases, verses or sections that keep standing out to you?

- Are there any that come to your mind even when you're *not* reading?

- If you identified anything in the last two questions, jot them down somewhere and spend some extra time praying about what God might be saying to you.

Notes & Prayers

Day 10

Today's Passage: Read *Philippians* and write a high-level outline of the main sections of *Philippians*.

When I say "high-level" I mean super high. This is not the detailed, multi-layer outline you hated doing in high school history class. This is more about taking something you are already familiar with – after reading it ten times! – to identify the major breaks in the book.

Remember the 1-paragraph summary from a couple of days ago? Think of this as the "next level" of breaking it down. Our minds learn – naturally and enjoyably – from the general to the specific. That's why it is so important to *not* jump too quickly into the details of verse-by-verse study.

What you create today is Step 1 in building the bridge from the general study of these first 15 days into the deeper study of the remaining weeks.

NOTE: If reading the word *outline* causes you to break into cold sweats, you can also simply journal about the book of *Philippians*. If you choose this option, use this as the "prompt" for your journal entry: *What are the major themes, sections, and flow of Philippians?*

For Reflection & Discussion

- Did you notice something new?

- Did something stand out to you that you had missed in previous readings?

- Did God solidify a truth or remind you of something?

Notes & Prayers

Day 11

Today's Passage: Read *Philippians*.

Today begins our final five days of "big picture" reading. Today is another day for simply "soaking" in God's Word.

Pray that God would meet you in what has now become familiar to you *and* show you something new. It doesn't have to be a specific "application" (although it certainly can be). It might be that you are drawn to worship or to give thanks. Or you might look at a relationship – a healthy one or a hard one – with fresh eyes. Or you might focus on a word, phrase, or theme.

Don't rush to get to the deep study. We will have many days to dive deep. Enjoy the journey. Enjoy "watching the play." A few days from now, we will begin to "study the acts and scenes."

For Reflection & Discussion

- What stood out to you today?

- What themes keep popping up that are beginning to cement in your mind?

- Ask God to bring a specific part (or a few parts) of *Philippians* to your mind throughout your day.

Notes & Prayers

Day 12

Today's Passage: Read *Philippians* as if you were a member of the church in Philippi, receiving this letter from Paul.

Imagine the first time this letter was read in the church in Philippi. Imagine gathering together with the other people in your church family, expecting to hear a word of encouragement, wisdom from the Old Testament, or some guidance for deepening your relationship with God or the people in your community.

Instead, one of the church leaders stands up and says, *"I had something I was going to share, but it can wait. Yesterday, a letter from our brother Paul was delivered. You've got to hear this!"*

The letter is read to the community. You hear these words, phrases, challenges, and encouragement for the very first time.

Imagine.

For Reflection & Discussion

- What comes to mind as you picture the scene?

- Did anything "sound" different to you as you read it today?

- What thoughts, ideas, or emotions would you like to carry forward with you into future readings of *Philippians*?

Notes & Prayers

DAY 13

Today's Passage: Read *Philippians* and do a Background Study on the *Audience* and the *Atmosphere*.

If you have a good study Bible, you probably have some of this info in your Bible. If not, there are many online resources available for free. You can simply search "free online study bible," or here are a couple of my favorites...

- https://biblia.com/books/csb/Php

- https://www.blueletterbible.org/csb/phl/1/1/t_comms_1104001

Getting even a little background will be so helpful, not to mention making the reading more enjoyable! As with Day 5 (the day we did the *Author* background study), this can be 10-15 minutes, or might turn into an hour or two!

Many people don't *think* they're going to enjoy background studies. After giving it a try, they come to realize how much better they understand and relate to the Bible when they have more context to what they are reading. Give it a try!

For Reflection & Discussion

- What did you discover about Philippi (and the people who lived there)?

- Did something stand out to you that you had missed in previous readings?

- Did God solidify a truth or remind you of something?

Notes & Prayers

Day 14

Today's Passage: Read *Philippians* in a different translation.

Pray the same prayer as on Day 9. Pray that God would meet you in the familiarity *and* show you something new.

You can return to one of the two translations you read on Day 4 or 9, or you can pick a fourth translation. On these days, it's ok to use a Bible app on your phone or tablet. (Make sure you turn off all notifications!)

For Reflection & Discussion

- What do you like – or not like – about today's translation? Did anything new stand out to you?

- Now that you're more familiar with this letter, what do you sense Paul's "mood" or "tone" was as he was writing?

- Are there any application points God keeps bringing to your mind? What is the first – or next – step you can take to make progress in that area?

Notes & Prayers

Day 15

Today's Passage: Read *Philippians*.

By now, you are quite familiar with *Philippians*. After all, you have read it more than a dozen times! You have read multiple translations. You have read it out loud. You have done some Background Studies. You have written an overview. You have created a basic outline.

Today is a day to soak...and celebrate.

Soak in this letter that – hopefully – has become a familiar, beloved companion.

Celebrate all that God is. Celebrate all that God has done. Celebrate who you are and what you have precisely *because* of who He is and what He has done.

And celebrate the progress you've made in your Bible reading. (After all, when was the last time you read an entire book of the Bible more than a dozen times?!)

Enjoy today.

For Reflection & Discussion

- What have these last 15 days been like for you? Fun? Insightful? Difficult? Challenging? Thought-provoking? (None of these are "right" or "wrong" answers, by the way.)

- What has stood out to you the most?

- What are you most looking forward to diving into a bit more deeply?

Notes & Prayers

Day 16

Today's Passage: *Philippians 1*

You have already read *Philippians* at least 15 times. As I mentioned earlier, these early days of the *Philippians Scripture Journey* are like watching a play many times. Over the next four days, we will be focusing on each "act" of the play. Starting on Day 20, we will explore each "scene."

Act 1 (or Chapter 1) could be called "The Joy of Partnership." Paul thanks the Philippian people for their partnership. He prays for his partners. He updates his partners. And he challenges his partners to live "worthy of the gospel."

God never intended for you to walk your journey of faith alone. We all need partners.

For Reflection & Discussion

- What stood out to you from this chapter?
- What did you find most encouraging?
- What did you find most challenging?
- Who are your "partners in the gospel?"

Notes & Prayers

Day 17

Today's Passage: *Philippians 2*

Act 2 (Chapter 2) could be called "Examples of Partnership." He begins with the call to look out for each other and set an example of Christlikeness. Then Paul points to Christ Himself – our perfect example.

He then moves on to show them what setting an example looks like. Finally, he wraps up this chapter with two living examples – Timothy and Epaphroditus.

When we look at the perfect example of Jesus – as well as the imperfect examples of other Christians seeking to honor Christ with their lives – we will be encouraged and better equipped to set an example for others.

For Reflection & Discussion

- What stood out to you from this chapter?
- What did you find most encouraging?
- What did you find most challenging?
- Who are the most Christlike examples in your life (past and present)?

Notes & Prayers

Day 18

Today's Passage: *Philippians 3*

Act 3 (Chapter 3) is all about "Partnering with Jesus." The first half is all about warnings. Warnings about the people who will discourage us or pull us away from focusing solely on Jesus. And warnings about our own pride, accomplishments, position, or heritage that are equally powerful (sometimes more powerful) distractions.

Paul then moves from warnings to reminders. Reminders to put knowing Christ ahead of everything else. Reminders of the heavenly calling of Christ Jesus. Reminders of the examples from within the community of faith. And a final reminder that our citizenship is not based on city, country, or even this planet. Our everlasting citizenship is heaven. Amen!

For Reflection & Discussion

- What stood out to you from this chapter?
- What did you find most encouraging?
- What did you find most challenging?
- Which of these warnings and reminders do you need most today?

Notes & Prayers

Day 19

Today's Passage: *Philippians 4*

The Final Act (Chapter 4) is "Partnering for the Long Haul." Were there relational challenges in the church (as there are today)? Yes. The call is to work through them. Are there times when we find ourselves anxious or concerned? Yes. Paul's reminder is that rejoicing, prayer, serve, gratitude, and God's nearness lead to peace.

Are there legitimate needs in the church? Yes. And we must all play our part and practice generosity to meet those needs. Are we the ultimate supplier of those needs? Not at all. That role belongs to God – *the One who will supply all our needs according to His glorious riches in Christ Jesus.*

Amen to that!

For Reflection & Discussion

- What stood out to you from this chapter?
- What did you find most encouraging?
- What did you find most challenging?
- Where do you look to find peace?
- In what areas do you trust God easily? Are there any you have trouble trusting God in? Why do you think you're lacking trust in that area?

Notes & Prayers

Day 20

Today's Passage: *Philippians 1:1-2*

Today we begin "studying the scenes" of the play we've been watching. You might want to bookmark this page because I am including some *General Questions* you can use every day. These questions are good ones to use anytime you are reading *any* Bible passage.

General Questions (for every day)

- What does this passage say about who God is?
- What does this passage say about what God has done?
- What does this passage say about your identity?
- What encourages you?
- What challenges you?
- What questions do you have?
- How will you respond?

It may seem strange to focus on the "greeting" for a full day. But look at how much is in there!

Take some time to think about (and even study) words like servant, saint, overseer, deacon, grace, and peace. Recognize how Paul identifies himself and the people he's writing to.

For Reflection & Discussion

- It's very common for Christians to use words like believer, follower, or even Christian. When was the last time you referred to yourself as a servant of Christ?

- How would thinking of other Christians as "saints" change how you treated or spoke to (or about) them?

- Spend some time thanking God for His gift of grace and peace.

Notes & Prayers

Day 21

Today's Passage: *Philippians 1:3-8*

What a powerful start to this letter! Imagine having someone write you a letter telling you how much they thank God for you. It would be so encouraging!

The reminder that follows is something you and I need – and rarely get. In a world that rewards performance above almost anything else, Paul reminds his readers (yes...that includes you) that we are all a work in progress.

God has begun something in you. God is working in you. God is carrying you. And God will complete what He began.

For Reflection & Discussion

- What has God begun in you? Are you confident that He will bring it to completion?

- Who are your "partners in grace?"

- Do you have someone you are thankful for? Write that letter!

Notes & Prayers

Day 22

Today's Passage: *Philippians 1:9-11*

I intentionally made the reading for today short, because I want you to spend more time praying than reading. I don't know about you, but I'm frequently better at *telling* people I'll pray for them than I am *actually praying* for them.

Paul not only tells people he's praying for them. He tells them exactly what he's praying. Look at all that Paul prays for in these three short verses:

>Their love may abound.

>Knowledge

>Depth of insight

>Discernment

>Purity and blamelessness

>The fruit of righteousness

>All would be to the glory and praise of God

Our relationships would be so different if we prayed this prayer for our family, friends, co-workers, and leaders (to name a few). Let's do it!

For Reflection & Discussion

- Is prayer a regular part of your daily life? How can you grow in that area?

- Using Paul's prayer as a model, spend some time praying for someone today. Then spend some time praying the same prayer for yourself.

Notes & Prayers

Day 23

Today's Passage: *Philippians 1:12-20*

The next three days could be read separately, or you could spend all three days reading verses 12-30. They both speak to Paul's perspective on the trials he is going through.

As a reminder, Paul is in prison. He *believes* that he will get out. But he doesn't *know* he will. And he certainly doesn't know *when*.

Paul could have chosen to focus on his circumstances. He could have chosen to focus on the uncertainty of his earthly future. He could have chosen to focus on the people (fellow believers by the way) who unjustly sought to make his life more difficult.

And yet, Paul chose to focus on Christ. Christ preached. Christ's Spirit. Christ's exaltation.

Keeping our eyes on Christ will help us navigate whatever challenges we face. Even the unjust ones.

For Reflection & Discussion

- What challenges are you currently facing?

- Are you more focused on your circumstance – or the actions of others – than you are on Christ?

- What is one way you can shift your focus onto Christ? (e.g. Reminders on your phone, internalizing Scripture, honest discussions with a trusted friend, etc.)

Notes & Prayers

Day 24

Today's Passage: *Philippians 1:21-26*

This is the second section (of three) where Paul gives us his perspective on his hardships. In the previous section, Paul declared his focus on Christ rather than his circumstances.

In today's verses, Paul takes it even further. He paints the seemingly worst-case scenario – his death in prison – as the ultimate best-case scenario. He reminds the Philippians, and us, that life in the body is a life for Christ. And life for all eternity is life with Christ.

For the Christian, there is no "worst-case." As long as we are in our earthly bodies, we have the opportunity to glorify Christ and serve others. At whatever time Christ calls us Home, we will rejoice as we experience Christ face-to-face, "which is far better indeed."

For Reflection & Discussion

- What does Paul's statement – "For to me, to live is Christ, and to die is gain" – mean to you?

- How often do you ponder eternity?

- How does the promise of eternity with Christ empower you to live more boldly in the present?

Notes & Prayers

Day 25

Today's Passage: *Philippians 1:27-30*

Two days ago, we looked at Paul's perspective on his sufferings and imprisonment. Yesterday we looked at facing our challenges in light of eternity. Today – still looking at how to endure hardships – Paul turns the focus outward.

Our perspective toward our circumstances is important. Living with our feet on earth and our eyes toward heaven is important. Not letting our circumstances keep us from serving others is also important.

In the midst of our suffering, we must conduct ourselves in a manner worthy of the gospel of Christ. In the midst of our suffering, we must stand firm alongside our fellow Christians. In the midst of our suffering, we must not give way to fear.

And finally, Paul's reminder that *"it has been granted to you on behalf of Christ not only to believe in Him, but also to suffer for Him"* sounds quite similar to what Christ told the disciples on the night He was betrayed...

"In the world you will have tribulation."

But don't forget the second part...

"But take courage; I have overcome the world!"

For Reflection & Discussion

- Do you stop serving others when you face challenges?

- How can you "contend side by side" with someone else who is struggling?

- How does knowing that suffering is part of the calling to follow Christ encourage – and challenge – you?

Notes & Prayers

Day 26

Today's Passage: *Philippians 2:1-4*

The first two verses of today's reading is an if/then statement. Actually, it's an if/if/if/if/then statement.

...*if* you have any encouragement in Christ... *if* any comfort from His love... *if* any fellowship with the Spirit... *if* any affection and compassion...*then* make my joy complete.

Paul spent the last few paragraphs looking at our approach to hard times. Now he gives some reminders of what we have as Christians – encouragement, comfort, fellowship, affection, compassion.

Our response? To make his joy complete *by being like-minded, having the same love, being united in spirit and purpose.*

The final two verses show us what it looks like if we live it out. Selfish ambition and empty pride are pushed away. Humility and serving others are embraced.

What a beautiful picture!

For Reflection & Discussion

- Which one of the "if" statements is easiest for you to embrace? Which is the hardest?

- What does it look like to be like-minded, have the same love and to be united in spirit and purpose?

- How might you push away selfish ambition and empty pride?

- How might you embrace humility and serve people around you?

Notes & Prayers

Day 27

Today's Passage: *Philippians 2:5-11*

While there are many well-known verses in *Philippians*, today's reading contains the most well-known *section*. Interestingly, we most often focus on either the first three verses or the last three. (For good reason. They're outstanding!)

The first three are all about the incarnation. The Creator of everything (see *John 1:3*) creates skin, then enters His own creation. Unfathomable!

The last three are a glimpse of Jesus in His rightful position. Exalted. In the highest place. Every knee bowed. Every tongue confessing. The Father glorified. Amazing!

We rarely talk about Verse 8 – the "transition verse."

> *"And being found in appearance as a man, He humbled Himself and became obedient to death – even death on a cross."*

Hold on! The Creator of the universe has entered His own creation...and then humbles Himself some more? Isn't the infinite Creator putting on skin humility enough?

If you and I are ever tempted to be prideful for even a moment, may we read this verse and be pulled toward humility once again.

For Reflection & Discussion

- What amazes you most about Christ's incarnation?
- Spend some time pondering a time when Jesus is on the Throne, every knee bows down, and every tongue confesses His lordship.
- How does Verse 8 inform your perspective on humility?

Notes & Prayers

DAY 28

Today's Passage: *Philippians 2:12-18*

Immediately after painting a clear picture of Jesus – in the flesh, humble, and glorified – Paul turns his readers' attention to the appropriate response. Work out your salvation.

Notice that Paul doesn't say "work *for* your salvation." He would never say that. After all, Paul is the one who wrote of salvation being by grace and not by works (*Ephesians 2:8-9*) and a gift we could never earn (*Romans 6:23*).

So then, what does he mean by "work out your salvation?"

You and I were given bodies at birth that are the same ones we will have our entire lives. Now, how we "work out" our physical bodies will have a significant impact on how well we live, heal, and serve.

Your salvation is a gift you will have for all eternity. Whether we "work out" our salvation will have a significant impact on how well we live, heal, and serve.

For Reflection & Discussion

- How could you "work out" your salvation?

- What would it look like "do everything without complaining or arguing?"

- How might you "shine as lights in the world" a little brighter today?

Notes & Prayers

Day 29

Today's Passage: *Philippians 2:19-30*

The first example Paul uses in this chapter is Jesus (Philippians 2:5-11). Beginning with Jesus's example is always a good idea!

Paul concludes the chapter with two more examples. Two people his readers would have known. Two people who weren't perfect. Two people with flaws *and* strengths.

The first is Timothy. Imagine the number of people Paul has met. And this is what he writes about Timothy,

> *"I have nobody else like him who will genuinely care for your needs."*

When it comes to "genuine care," Paul wants his readers to look at the example of Christlike care Timothy shows.

And finally, we read about Epaphroditus, someone who only shows up in Philippians. We know almost nothing about him. What *do* we know?

The church in Philippi had taken a collection and needed someone to take the journey and deliver it to Paul. Epaphroditus raised his hand.

He saw a need. He realized he could meet the need. And he met it. Sounds like something we should do as well, don't you think?

For Reflection & Discussion

- Who are the Christlike examples in your life?

- Who do you know who shows "genuine care" for people?

- What is a current need you know you can meet? How could you meet it?

Notes & Prayers

Day 30

Today's Passage: *Philippians 3:1-9*

Our culture thrives on credentials and comparison. What's your degree? What's your title? What's your heritage? What's your experience? Where do you live? What do you own?

And the list goes on.

Paul had it all. He was from the "best" tribe. He had the "highest" education. He had the "right" job. He had lived the "perfect" (externally) life.

His assessment? Rubbish. It was all rubbish. By the way, the literal translation of the Greek word *skybala* is "dung." Yup. You get the picture.

Paul had the credentials to out-compare anyone. But compared to knowing Christ? It's all dung.

For Reflection & Discussion

- What "credentials" are you most likely to flaunt?

- Do you get trapped in the comparison game?

- How can you prioritize knowing Jesus above everything else?

Notes & Prayers

Day 31

Today's Passage: *Philippians 3:10-16*

Look at the phrases Paul uses immediately following his words about putting knowing Christ above everything else.

> "...*I press on to take hold* of that for which Christ Jesus took hold of me."

> "...*straining* toward what is ahead..."

> "...*I press on toward the goal* to win the prize of God's heavenly calling in Christ Jesus."

> "...we must *live up to* what we have already attained."

Salvation is a gift. We can't earn a relationship with Jesus. But let us never forget that growing in that relationship – as with any other relationship – will take effort.

And that effort will be worth it. For today. For tomorrow. And for eternity.

For Reflection & Discussion

- How have you shared in Christ's suffering?

- How are you pressing on, straining, and living up to your calling? How can you improve in this area?

- Have you ever had a difference of opinion about a spiritual matter that was eventually resolved? What was the process like? Are you experiencing anything like that now?

Notes & Prayers

DAY 32

Today's Passage: *Philippians 3:17-4:3*

When it comes to living God-honoring relationships within the faith community, Paul covers four extremely important facets in eight verses.

Be careful who you follow. It is important to look for godly examples. The world is full of ungodly examples. We will become like those we surround ourselves with.

Live in light of eternity. We certainly need to be present in our work, relationships, and life here on earth. And yet, the perspective that gives us freedom and boldness is heavenly. This world is not our home. Let's not forget that.

Reconcile whenever possible. Paul gives us no details about the conflict between Euodia and Syntyche. That's a good thing, because we would likely compare our situation to theirs. What Paul does provide is a call to reconcile. Maybe that's because forgiveness and reconciliation is the clearest earthly picture we have of what Jesus's death and resurrection has done for us.

Partner together. No one is equipped to live the abundant life Jesus offers without help from others. We need each other. We need to not only offer help. We need to accept it. (Go ahead and read this paragraph again. It's too important to miss.)

For Reflection & Discussion

- What examples are you following that you shouldn't be?
- How can you live with a "heaven is my home" perspective?
- Is there anyone you need to reconcile with? What's your first, or next, step?
- Do you struggle more with offering help or accepting it?

Notes & Prayers

Day 33

Today's Passage: *Philippians 4:4-9*

Smack dab in the middle of today's reading is the second most popular – and quoted out of context – passage in *Philippians*. (Don't worry, we will look at the most-quoted-out-of-context verse tomorrow.)

Anytime someone is going through a hard time or personal trial, someone will quote Philippians 4:6-7:

> "Be anxious for nothing, but in everything, by prayer and petition, with thanksgiving, present your requests to God. Don't worry about anything, but in everything, through prayer and petition with thanksgiving, present your requests to God. And the peace of God, which surpasses all understanding, will guard your hearts and your minds in Christ Jesus."

Beginning with "*Don't be anxious*" (without the two verses that precede this statement) and ending with "*the peace of God will guard your hearts and minds*" (without the two verses that follow) is to tell someone to do something without showing them how, and promising peace without showing them how to sustain it.

Verses 4-5 encourage us to rejoice. To give thanks. To strive, in the middle of the storm, to show gentleness and graciousness. And to remember that "*The Lord is near.*"

It is a heart strengthened by gratitude, a life lived with gentle grace, and a constant reminder of God's nearness that make it possible to "*be anxious for nothing.*"

And how to do we sustain God's peace? By thinking, dwelling, and meditating on that which is good and true. And by following the lead of people (like Paul) who experienced and modeled peace in the midst of suffering.

For Reflection & Discussion

- What can you rejoice about today?
- In what areas of life do you need to live with more gentleness and graciousness?
- How can you remind yourself that "*the Lord is near*"?
- What prayers and petitions do you need to present to God?
- What do you "dwell/think/meditate" on? What *should* you?
- Who do you know who models peace in the midst of the storm? What can you learn and model from their lives?

Notes & Prayers

Day 34

Today's Passage: *Philippians 4:10-20*

Other than John 3:16, today's reading contains probably the most quoted verse in the entire Bible.

"I can do all things through Christ who gives me strength."

How many times have you thought about that verse? How many times have you said that verse? How many times have you thought about the *context* of that verse?

The context of this is receiving help from others, combined with living in contentment.

Taken out of context, it sounds like a very self-focused verse. If I have Christ in me, then I can do anything.

And yet, Paul is talking to his fellow Christians in Philippi who have helped him. They have provided for his needs. They have prayed for him. They have sent him help again and again.

He's more focused on them than he is on himself.

He also writes of being content. Content with a lot. Content with a little. Content with abundance. Content with need.

Contentment isn't about being lazy or lacking ambition. (After all, you would be hard-pressed to find someone who has worked harder or "pressed on" more than Paul!)

Contentment is about recognizing the truth that God has surrounded you with the community of faith and His very presence – no matter what our circumstances may be!

For Reflection & Discussion

- Spend some time pondering your own "contentment level."
- Where are you experiencing abundance? Where are you experiencing need?
- Whom has God surrounded you with?
- Do you believe – at your core – that verse 19 is true? If so, may verse 20 be your prayer of proclamation today!

Notes & Prayers

Day 35

Today's Passage: *Philippians 4:21-23*

Paul wraps up this letter similarly to how he started it. Focused on people. Focused on his people. His faith community. His partners in the gospel.

He sends them greetings from himself. He sends them greetings from his travel companions.

And then he blesses them. A reminder and offering of *"the grace of the Lord Jesus Christ"* is a blessing.

The second verse of this letter is a blessing. The final verse of this letter is a blessing.

Remind yourself of the blessing provided by both community and grace today. Then find someone you can bless with a reminder of the Lord's grace toward them.

For Reflection & Discussion

- Who are the people that have been your "partners in grace?"

- How could you thank – letter, email, text – the people you identified in the first question?

- Have you ever pondered the difference between a prayer and blessing?

- Do you need to receive the Lord's grace today? (He's already given it. Go ahead and *accept* it.)

- Is there someone you could offer grace to today?

Notes & Prayers

Day 36

Today's Passage: *Philippians 1*

For the final five days of the *Philippians Scripture Journey*, we are going to "widen the lens" as we did in the first several days. We have been looking at the "scenes" of the play. Now we will spend a day returning to each of the four "acts." Our final day will be spent "watching the play."

Since it will only take you a few minutes to read this chapter, read it at least twice. Ideally, reading it 3-4 times in 3-4 different translations will provide great insight. It will also help you slow down enough to hear what God might be saying to you today.

The primary reflection and discussion questions for each day will be the same. I have also provided the days when we looked at each chapter throughout our journey so you can easily find them if you would like to revisit the more specific questions and your earlier responses.

For Reflection & Discussion

- What does today's passage have to say about who God is?
- What does today's passage have to say about what God has done?
- What does today's passage have to say about who I am?
- What is my response? (This could be an application, a question, a time of silence, worship, etc.)
- For deeper reflection you can look back at the *Reflection & Discussion* questions from Days 16 and 20-25.

Notes & Prayers

Day 37

Today's Passage: *Philippians 2*

As with yesterday, I recommend reading this chapter 3-4 times – or listening to it – in several different translations. The different word and phrase choices always bring fresh insight to a passage.

For these days, I will provide very little "teaching" about each chapter. You have now read this book many times all the way through and studied it deeply. Spend these days talking to God about what He has already shown you and how He would have you live out what you've discovered.

Make sure to also spend some time in silence, listening to what He might still have for you that you haven't noticed before!

For Reflection & Discussion

- What does today's passage have to say about who God is?

- What does today's passage have to say about what God has done?

- What does today's passage have to say about who I am?

- What is my response? (This could be an application, a question, a time of silence, worship, etc.)

- For deeper reflection you can look back at the *Reflection & Discussion* questions from Days 17 and 26-29.

Notes & Prayers

Day 38

Today's Passage: *Philippians 3*

Once again, I encourage you to read this chapter multiple times in multiple translations. Pay attention to subtle differences and what is emphasized by those differences.

You'll find warnings against false teachers, Paul's "credentials" (which he considered *dung* compared to Christ), and a calling to press on toward the goal. Reading this in multiple translations on the same day will give you a fresh perspective and appreciate for what Paul is saying.

If you haven't been reading out loud, give it a try. You will notice different words, phrases, and ideas. You will remember it better. And you will be able to focus more fully as well.

Reflection & Discussion

- What does today's passage have to say about who God is?
- What does today's passage have to say about what God has done?
- What does today's passage have to say about who I am?
- What is my response? (This could be an application, a question, a time of silence, worship, etc.)
- For deeper reflection you can look back at the *Reflection & Discussion* questions from Days 18 and 30-32.

Notes & Prayers

Day 39

Today's Passage: *Philippians 4*

One final day, I would encourage you to read this chapter several times, in different translations each time. Read out loud. You might even want to listen to it a few times as you take a walk, do some work around the house, or drive in your car.

Ask God for fresh eyes. Ask God to bring His Word to your mind throughout the day. Ask God to remind you of what is true (in a world with very loud lies).

Ask God to *shape* you by what He has *shown* you.

For Reflection & Discussion

- What does today's passage have to say about who God is?

- What does today's passage have to say about what God has done?

- What does today's passage have to say about who I am?

- What is my response? (This could be an application, a question, a time of silence, worship, etc.)

- For deeper reflection you can look back at the *Reflection & Discussion* questions from Days 19 and 33-35.

Notes & Prayers

DAY 40

Today's Passage: *Philippians*

Our journey in Paul's wonderful letter to the church in Philippi comes to an end today. Do not let *your* journey with *Philippians* end today. I pray that you return to it again and again.

Several years from now, you could pull out this book and go on another 40-day journey. You could also use this simple concept – Watch the play. Explore the acts. Study the scenes. – to do a shorter or longer study of *Philippians*.

As we finish, my prayer for you is the same as the one Paul began with...

> "*And this is my prayer: that your love may abound more and more in knowledge and depth of insight, so that you may be able to test and prove what is best and may be pure and blameless for the day of Christ, filled with the fruit of righteousness that comes through Jesus Christ, to the glory and praise of God.*" Philippians 1:9-11

Alongside,

For Reflection & Discussion

- What stood out to you today as you revisited *Philippians* as a whole?

- What is your biggest takeaway from the *Philippians Scripture Journey*?

- What are some topics, themes, sections, phrases, etc. that you want to study more deeply?

- Are there any verses or paragraphs you want to internalize and carry with you?

Notes & Prayers

About the Author

Am I the only one who thinks it is a little bit strange that the "About the Author" page is typically the only page in an entire book written in the third person? After all, I am the author. I am writing this page. It feels a bit weird to write about myself in the third person.

So let's try this...

I, Keith Ferrin, am an author, speaker, storyteller, and messaging coach. My passion is helping individuals, families, and entire church communities move from "should" to "want" when it comes to reading the Bible. I believe the Bible isn't just true, but it's also awesome! When I'm not the one on stage, I'm typically helping coach the people who are. I love to help C-level leaders, teams, pastors and entrepreneurs simplify their messages and deliver them well.

Actually, I guess all that is more of what I "do." As far as who I am...I am a disciple of Jesus Christ, a husband to Kari (world's most outstanding wife), and a father to Sarah, Caleb, and Hannah (the three coolest – and craziest – kids on the planet).

In case you are still reading...I am also a coffee drinker, ice cream eater, amateur guitar player, lover of twisty-turny movies, and eater of almost any kind of food (except olives).

If you're looking for me, head on up to Seattle. I will be the happy guy hanging out with his wife and kids doing something outside. Unless, of course, it is family movie night. Then we'll be inside.

A Few of My Other Books

All of my books are available on Amazon. If you're buying multiple copies, bulk discounts are available at www.keithferrin.com

The Scripture Journey Series

Gospel of John Scripture Journey – Who better to walk us the life, teaching, death and resurrection of Jesus than one of the twelve disciples? John refers to himself as simply "the one Jesus loved." After a journey through John's gospel you will not only see why he refers to himself that way. You will realize that "loved" describes yourself as well.

Acts Scripture Journey – Take a journey through the first few decades of the early church. Jesus has walked the earth, died, and risen. *Acts* opens with Jesus's ascension into heaven. The Luke (the author) takes us first-hand through the first followers of Jesus, the lives of Peter, James, John, and the missionary journeys of the Apostle Paul.

Ephesians Scripture Journey – When it comes to living out our faith, the temptation is to make it all about morality – doing the *right* things and avoiding the *wrong* things. In Paul's letter to the *Ephesians*, he takes a different approach altogether. Paul's letter to the Church in Ephesus will remind you of your identity in Christ, so you can live with greater freedom, boldness, authenticity, and purpose.

Colossians Scripture Journey – Are you tempted to view "Bible times" as a culture we can't relate to today? Paul's letter to the church in Colossae shows us just how similar our culture is to theirs. Paul combines the knowledge of a theologian, the truth-telling of a good friend, and the heart of a parent to encourage his readers – and us – to not only believe in Jesus, but to grow each day in understanding, faith, and obedience.

2 Timothy Scripture Journey – What would you write if you were in prison, on Death Row, knowing you were experiencing your final days on earth, and you were writing a letter to someone you had mentored, who was now one of your best friends? That's exactly the situation Paul was in when he wrote 2 Timothy...his final letter. Paul writes about hardships and suffering. He writes about living out your calling. He writes about God's faithfulness. He writes about Christ's example. He writes about fleeing evil. He writes about pursuing good. And the list goes on and on..

Hebrews Scripture Journey – In this study, you will discover the significance of Christ as the ultimate High Priest, perfect sacrifice, and mediator of a new covenant. You will uncover the richness of God's redemptive plan, rooted in the Old Testament and fulfilled in Jesus. You will anchor your faith in unchanging promises, find the strength to run life's race, and embrace a life fully devoted to God.

1 Peter Scripture Journey – Living out a life that honors Jesus is hard. Really hard. Our culture doesn't encourage it. In fact, in so many ways, it opposes it. Peter's first letter is filled with encouragement and guidance to help us walk the path of pursuing holiness in a world that pushes us to do the opposite. His call to live holy lives is surrounded by reminders of God's goodness, faithfulness, and never-ending presence.

Advent Scripture Journey – Too often, the days and weeks leading up to Christmas Morning are filled with busyness. We're busy shopping. We're busy wrapping. We're busy cooking. We're busy with parties. We're busy with friends and family. This December, take a few minutes each day to go on a journey. A journey through the whole Bible, beginning on Page 1 and taking you to the manger. To pause. To remember. To reflect. To be fully present. To worship.

Lent Scripture Journey – As you prepare for Easter, the *Lent Scripture Journey* will be your daily guide from Ash Wednesday through Easter Morning. While some Lenten devotionals focus only on the final week – from the Triumphal Entry to Resurrection Morning – the *Lent Scripture Journey* takes you through the full life of Jesus. After all, Jesus's birth, life, teaching, miracles, suffering and crucifixion were all pointing to the glory of the empty grave!

How to Enjoy Reading Your Bible

Do you enjoy the Bible? If we enjoy the Bible, we will read it. If we enjoy it, we'll talk about it. If we enjoy it, consistency won't be a problem. After almost three decades of speaking and writing, I have compiled my "Top 10 Tips" for enjoying the Bible. Tips that are applicable immediately. Written using stories, analogies, and common language, these tips are equally accessible for someone who is exploring, is new to faith in Jesus, or has been hanging out with Jesus for decades. If you want to enjoy the Bible – I wrote this book for you. Because believing it's true is not enough.

Like Ice Cream: The Scoop on Helping the Next Generation Fall in Love with God's Word

What if passing on a love for God's Word could be as natural – and enjoyable – as passing on a love for ice cream? I believe it can be. When it comes to helping the next generation fall in love with the Bible, the principles are surprisingly similar to the way a love for ice cream gets passed on from generation to generation. Whether you are a parent, grandparent, youth pastor – or anyone who cares deeply about the next generation – you will find *Like Ice Cream* filled with encouragement and practical ideas you can start using today.

Falling in Love with God's Word

This book will help you discover what God always intended Bible study to be. God wants you to understand His Word. He wants you to enjoy your time in His Word. He wants you to remember what you read in His Word. In this book, I walk you through my entire process for deeply studying a book of the Bible. My prayer is this book will transform your Bible study time in a way that will allow God to use His Word to transform you!

Rapid Bible Read Thru

Have you ever read through the whole Bible? Have you ever started...only to stop after a few weeks? Do you wish you understood the Bible better? Do you long to know The Author more deeply? If so, *Rapid Bible Read Thru* is just what you need!

Is it a challenge? *Yes.* It is easier than most people think? *Absolutely.* Will it transform your understanding of the Bible and deeper your relationship with God? *No doubt!* This book will walk you step-by-step through the Why, What, and How of doing a *Rapid Bible Read Thru*.

Bible Praying for Parents

As parents, we want to pray for our kids. We know we should pray for them. And yet, our prayers often feel repetitive. So then, how do we know what to pray? How do we know we are covering every aspect of their lives (rather than only what's urgent at the moment)? The answer is *Bible Praying*. After all, when we pray God's Word, we pray God's will.

I wrote this book with my friend Judy Fetzer, who introduced me to praying the words of Scripture for our children. In this book we've turned 365 Bible passages (in 20+ categories) into prayer. We've also included a section of *Bible Blessings* straight from God's Word.

BIBLE TOOLBOX

Bible Toolbox is the world's first "Guided AI" tool specifically designed for Bible study. I co-created it with my friend CJ McDaniel, the founder and CEO of Adazing (a software company that creates writing and marketing tools and training for authors).

Think of it as the power of AI with "guard rails." Using the ease of drop-down menus and simple prompts, *Bible Toolbox* allows you to do never-before-possible research in a fraction of the time – and at a fraction of the cost of other software tools or books.

Whether you have a lot of experience with technology or none at all, *Bible Toolbox* will guide you each step of the way!

Here are just a handful of things *Bible Toolbox* can do:

- Historical & Cultural Context
- In-Depth Verse Analysis
- Word and Phrase Studies
- Character or Topical Studies
- Sermon Prep (Research and Brainstorming Analogies and Illustrations)
- Family Devotions
- Reading & Prayer Plans
- Historical & Cultural Context
- Application Points
- Built-In Tools for Churches (social media, job descriptions, video scripts, etc.)
- And heaps more!

Visit www.keithferrin.com/bibletoolbox for a special discount since you purchased this book!

Let's Connect!

I love to connect with my readers. Truly. Shoot me an email. I'll write back.

While there are several ways we can connect, here are the easiest ones to start with...

- Email: keith@keithferrin.com
- Website: www.keithferrin.com
- YouTube ("Your Bible Coach"): www.youtube.com/@keithferrin

You can also find me using @KeithFerrin on pretty much any social media platform.

amazon.com/author/keithferrin

youtube.com/keithferrin

instagram.com/keithferrin

facebook.com/keithferrin

pinterest.com/keithferrin

in
linkedin.com/in/keithferrin/

If you have a question or comment, please shoot me a note. Most of the videos I create on YouTube, books I write, or resources I create come from suggestions or questions I hear from my readers.

So...fire away. I'd love to hear from you.

Alongside,

Keith

Made in the USA
Columbia, SC
01 October 2024